Sustaining Faith in School Leadership

Alan Flintham
Chaplain, Derby Cathedral

GROVE BOOKS LIMITED
RIDLEY HALL RD CAMBRIDGE CB3 9HU

Contents

Acknowledgments

I would like to express my grateful thanks to Alison Farnell, Gillian Georgiou and Emily Norman who have so conscientiously supervised and supported my writing of this booklet. Most particular thanks, however, are due to the school leaders who were interviewed and whose practitioner voice so illuminates the text.

First Impression January 2022
ISSN 2041–0964
ISBN 978 1 78827 213 1

Sustaining Faith

'Faith gives substance to our hopes.' Hope as an important component of
school leadership and how it can be sustained in practice was the subject of a
previous Grove booklet.[1] Using the metaphor of 'reservoirs of hope,' it argued
that school leaders, particularly when faced with challenging circumstances
and critical incidents, are called to act as the 'external reservoir of hope' for
their community, by the way they exercise spiritual and moral leadership in
confronting and surmounting those challenges.[2] To do this, the school leader
must draw upon individual reserves of self-belief and resilience, a personal
'internal reservoir of hope.' And that reservoir demands solid foundations:
foundations of faith.

Whilst faith as such is not usually their regular topic of discussion, it is difficult to find a school leader in whatever context who, if approached, cannot
readily articulate the ethical and moral base on which they stand. This 'faith'
(although many will not call it that) is clearly founded on a set of consistent
core values and provides a sustaining inner resource when applying these
in action.

This book explores how faith itself, however defined, can be sustained in
school leaders and how, in turn, it can provide a sustaining foundation for
leadership actions. It draws on interviews with serving school leaders in a
variety of contexts and captures their authentic practitioner voice. It seeks
to support Christian school leaders working in schools that face challenging circumstances (arguably all schools, in some sense). By articulating their
experiences and motivations, an aim of the book is also to encourage and
secure future vocations to such roles and to inform those who select for them.

The aim is that its remit is not simply restricted to those working in and with
church schools—its message is applicable to all school leaders of faith, being
widely defined to encompass all who can identify and articulate the moral
and ethical base which underpins their leadership actions. It is written for
all who have faith in a vision of education that is predicated on hope, who
hold on to their hope of the prospect of a better future and who are prepared

to work towards it. For hope provides the essential resource for renewal and regeneration, for repentance and reconciliation.

Hope is one of the four basic elements in what has been described as 'a long-term educational ecology: wisdom, hope, community and dignity,' articulated in the *Church of England Vision for Education*. It is a vision which is avowedly 'deeply Christian, with the promise by Jesus of life in all its fullness at its heart.'[3] But although, in Church of England schools, the working out of that vision 'will be seen explicitly in teaching and learning…and also in the authentically Christian worship and ethos of those schools,' it is not confined to those schools. For it is clearly recognized that: 'In other schools not rooted in an explicit Christian ethos, our vision for education can still be expressed and promoted as one of human flourishing that can inspire what the school is and does.'[4] It is a vision for the common good, hospitable to diversity, respectful of freedom and inviting collaboration between all those who would describe themselves as 'school leaders of faith.'

Varieties of Faith

Faith comes in many shapes and sizes, and individual faith journeys can begin and develop very differently. For some leaders, their ethical base is firmly linked to—and reinforced by—active religious practice as a member of a particular faith community; for others it is one in which faith may have become more of a state of 'believing without belonging.'[5] Yet for others, whilst any motivational connection between religious beliefs and their own ethical value system may have long since been broken or indeed never have existed, adherence to a philosophy of 'Do as you would be done by' still remains their guiding principle. However, for the school leader who is a Christian, whether serving in a church school or secular context, their belief is in the God who reveals himself in Jesus Christ and calls them not only to love God but also into loving service towards their neighbour.

> **For the Christian school leader their belief is in the God who reveals himself in Jesus Christ**

Cooling has argued that 'People can cooperate in achieving educational goals even though they might hold conflicting beliefs…The way forward is for people's religious and non-religious beliefs to be treated as a resource in the cause of promoting the common good.'[6] He therefore accepts that 'Staff selection for faith schools on the basis of religious philosophy is appropriate as long as commitment to the goals of public education is maintained and the diversity of society as a whole is reflected.'[7] Collectively, school leaders within such schools of a religious character bring to their roles a variety of nuanced religious or secular philosophies and, by so doing, reflect the diversity of society as a whole. School leadership is underpinned, consciously or subconsciously, overtly or covertly, by a leader's worldview, which may be religious or non-religious. Such worldviews 'can be relatively straightforward, with clear boundaries expressed through institutional belonging, or they can be complex, fluid and woven together from a number of perspectives.'[8] Yet that very plurality, across a wide spectrum of belief and a variety of contexts, provides a rich collective resource from which to develop and secure a greater commonality of shared values, irrespective of provenance.

Farnell has identified a simple spectrum of religious beliefs amongst the leaders of Church of England schools, ranging across: 'humanist with values shared with Christianity'; 'people from faiths other than Christianity'; 'varieties of cultural Christian' with some heritage of Christian belief; to those who firmly identify as 'practising Christians.'[9] An alternative but complementary taxonomy across a wider range of school contexts can be used to describe these various faith positions as: *intra-faith*—being linked to a particular religious tradition, with leadership in a school reflecting the religious character of that tradition; *or interfaith*—exercising leadership in a school of a different religious tradition to that subscribed to personally.[10] But there are also those who may well be still active within their faith communities but feel called to work out their faith through service in the *extra-faith* context of the secular school environment. Finally there are those who self-identify as being of *no faith*, some of whom, whilst no longer active in any profession of religious faith, are content to be described as 'cultural Christians.' They still retain the essence of the basic tenets of Christian belief and its value system laid down in childhood, but this has subsequently been moderated and developed into a non-theistic or humanist morality.

Varieties of Service

This taxonomy of faith positions was tested by interviewing a sample of thirty school leaders reflecting different facets of faith and varieties of contexts.[11] They represented a cross-section of schools in different social and geographical contexts across England, drawn equally from the primary and secondary sectors. Their individual personal faith perspectives drew from the Anglican (9), Roman Catholic (9), Jewish (3), Muslim (2), Buddhist (1), Methodist (1), Hindu (1), Sikh (1), charismatic Christian (1) and Humanist (2) traditions. Some seventeen were leaders of schools of the particular religious tradition congruent with their own faith perspective (including a charismatic Christian family who had set up a faith-based home school for their own children). Six others exercised interfaith leadership roles in schools of a different religious character from their own faith perspective (including a Roman Catholic head teacher of a Jewish secondary school, an Anglican head teacher of a Muslim secondary school and an Anglican head teacher of a Methodist primary school, together with two head teachers of joint Roman Catholic-Anglican secondary schools and a Humanist leading a newly-founded Church of England secondary school). Seven were leaders operating purely within the extra-faith secular school environment. All, however, were content to be described as 'school leaders of faith,' even though that faith perspective and the context in which it was exercised varied considerably.

The Bible teaches that 'There are varieties of gifts, but the same Spirit; there are varieties of service but the same Lord' (1 Cor 12.4–5). Varieties of faith, of gifts and of service can be found represented in the leadership of all schools. The following chapter will draw on interview data to consider how that variety is demonstrated in leadership motivation and practice. This leadership not only exemplifies the fundamental components of wisdom, hope, community and dignity identified within the *Church of England Vision for Education*, but also reflects the educational purpose of the leader who, to use the terminology of Ford and Wolfe, is *Called, Connected, Committed*.[12] Such leaders are *called* through a strong sense of personal vocation, *connected* in networks of mutual support to securing 'a vision of human flourishing for all,' and *committed* in clarity of purpose and resilience to delivering it in the face of contextual challenge.[13]

Questions for Reflection

- Where would you locate yourself on a spectrum of faith within the context of your service?

- How would your staff, pupils and school community *know* this from your leadership practice?

- What advantages do you feel accrue from your position on this spectrum? Are there any evident downsides? If so, how do you seek to overcome them?

Confronting Challenge

> So faith by itself, if it has no works, is dead.
>
> (Jas 2.17)

Irrespective of faith position and context of service, many school leaders of faith would identify with the Called, Connected, Committed terminology devised by Ford and Wolfe. They would echo that sense of being called 'to articulate a strong sense of personal vocation and to demonstrate this through their words, actions and decision making, exemplifying moral purpose, confident vision, and ambitious trajectory of improvement.' They would value the opportunity to draw support from being connected 'within communities of practice and networks of mutual support, positioning themselves within positive relationships that sustain and encourage all parties.' They would seek to remain committed to being 'clear about their purpose and resilient in the face of challenge.'[14] They would often be made very aware of the cost of confronting that challenge, when difficult decisions have to be made and maintained against the odds, and when faith is judged not in its words but by its works.

Nowhere has that costly challenge been more significantly faced than in confronting the pressures of the pandemic emergency of 2020–2021 on the continued effective provision of education. In the midst of that time, the Archbishops of Canterbury and York issued a letter to the nation calling on all to be committed to being 'calm, courageous and compassionate' in the face of continued crisis.[15] These attributes were particularly required of school leaders who found themselves facing: 'seemingly impossible decisions with pressure from both sides…as they wrestle with deeply complex problems where no easy solutions are available.'[16] Such pressures clearly required school leaders to remain personally 'called, connected and committed.'

Called

Being called is shown in a strong sense of personal vocation, demonstrated in words and actions which are clearly based on moral purpose. For the leaders interviewed, that calling was often to service in a specific context, be it to a school of a particular faith tradition, or a particularly socially challenged area. Some who felt called to exercise a leadership role in an intra-faith context (that is, in a school linked to their own personal faith perspective) expressed the view that 'here I can live out my faith and fulfil a duty to make that faith accessible to others.' This was possible in a situation where it was felt there was 'no cognitive dissonance' between a personal belief system and the espoused values of the school. However, it was accepted that such cognitive dissonance could arise, for example in dealing with tension between a personal philosophy that 'all are of infinite worth as children of God' and negative parental pressure about the admission of traveller children to an oversubscribed church school, serving an affluent suburban area.

For those operating in the interfaith environment, there was a sense of fulfilment arising from utilizing the 'creative tension rather than cognitive dissonance' of two faiths working together in joint provision, where different perspectives 'disturbed comfortableness,' caused re-evaluation of essentials and honed 'a faith capable of jumping out into the unknown.' It was felt to be 'easier to understand people of faith if you are a person of faith (even a different one) yourself.' Thus, for such leaders operating 'beyond the comfort zone,' there was a need for an explicitly declared framework of faith-based values within the school. As one such interfaith leader put it: 'I couldn't be head of this school if it didn't have a faith background (even if it is different to my own). I need an explicit morality, not morality behind a mask.' But that morality does not have to be explicitly based in a religious tradition. An experienced head teacher with a personal humanist perspective felt called away from leadership of a secular school toward the foundation headship of a Church of England school because of 'the congruence of values of compassion, tolerance and social justice which are not exclusively religious but which are simply the cornerstones of a well-rounded education wherever it is set.' He relished the opportunity to apply that philosophy to the blank canvas of a new school.

Those working in secular environments as extra-faith leaders also felt that this was where they were called or meant to be. Such feelings might be expressed in the language of faith: 'God's call to me to be a servant leader' in a challenging comprehensive school, or described in secular terms as the opportunity of service to a local area long known and loved. For some with a particular faith perspective, there was a realistic recognition that leadership in a school linked to that tradition could result in unsustainable tensions between a personal liberal faith perspective, sitting somewhat loosely to the tenets of the tradition, and the expectations of the authority structures of the faith community. In such a situation, it was felt better to accept the challenge of the secular post, whilst remaining comfortable in yourself, in the belief that it was still God's purpose that this role was accepted.

But there is also a wider sense of being called to be 'an oasis of calm when crisis strikes,' mitigating the pressures of keeping staff and pupils safe, reassuring and supporting parents, and maintaining (as much as possible) some semblance of normality: a leadership situation described by one school leader as 'like being on a knife edge the whole time.' And all this whilst having the courage to take, and stand by, difficult decisions, with the compassion to support those bruised by them, whilst still striving to maintain the personal equanimity and self-belief secured by standing on the firm foundations of the leader's own faith.

Connected

To maintain and reinforce that sense of calling, and to find calm reassurance in the face of challenge, it is necessary to be connected through networks of support. These provide not only communities of professional practice but, more importantly, create positive personal relationships, with opportunities to step back and see the wood for the trees within a secure, mutually supportive environment. Such networks provide vehicles to offer compassionate support to fellow leaders facing difficult situations. They offer forums where courageous decisions can first be contemplated in a non-judgmental setting. It has been argued elsewhere that these networks can be characterized as: belief networks, where support for one's value system and the leadership actions emanating from it can be drawn from colleagues felt to be on the same page; support networks, from within the family or the church community; and external networks, providing the opportunity to switch off from the demands of leadership and become immersed in something completely different.[17]

To maintain that sense of calling it is necessary to be connected through networks of support

Networks of peer support, from colleagues in similar contexts or facing similar circumstances, are not restricted to the specific faith sector but draw from the common context of the universal nature of school leadership. But for the intra-faith school leader, there was also reinforcement from 'the shared faith of senior staff and the governing body walking with me [which] provided feedback, affirmation and encouragement in self-belief.' For the interfaith or extra-faith leader, their own worshipping community could provide 'quiet support and affirmation as well as spiritual sustenance in my practice of faith.' It offered affirming knowledge that 'people who know me are praying for me and my work'; others, however, expressed 'the need for anonymity so I can pray and be myself' and not simply be perceived in a leadership role.

For those not active in a religious tradition, professional networks could be supplemented by a close relationship with a trusted colleague on the same wavelength, and able to be 'more than a mentor, more than a professional listening partner, [providing] the cathartic spiritual support of a soul friend.'

However, for leaders with a theocentric faith, there is a greater level of connectedness beyond that offered by professional networks, namely connectedness with God. Schumacher has identified mechanisms for connectedness within the Christian faith tradition, drawing on the spiritual disciplines of solitude, simplicity and Sabbath, which can be explored even when networks of professional support are unavailable or inadequate.[18] She identifies solitude as 'a state of mind and heart' which helps cultivate an inward attentiveness; simplicity as 'learning to let go' of the detail to cultivate the ability to focus on essentials; and Sabbath rest as a 'time for being in the midst of a life of doing.' One school leader interviewed spoke of securing 'solitude' through 'micro-retreat': wilfully arriving early for meetings, parking up on the riverbank opposite County Hall with mobile switched off, and there finding reflective space, 'just me and my God.' Another spoke of 'simplicity,' secured by stripping away the details of a problem to reveal its bare moral essentials, and then asking: 'what would Jesus do?' A third stressed the importance of preserving space away from school work through 'a day of rest for worship and walking, reflecting and renewing,' in order to recharge for the stresses of the week ahead. For many school leaders of religious faith, such reflective practices, which permit constructive introspection and space for a closer relationship with God, can help maintain their spiritual resilience, making leadership 'more a condition of the heart than a set of things to do.'[19]

> **Reflective practices help maintain spiritual resilience**

Committed

Commitment is shown through maintaining clarity of purpose and resilience in the face of challenge, when the rhetoric of faith is confronted by messy realities. Those realities could range from high-level critical incidents, such as the death of a member of the school community, to the day-to-day pressures, 'when every day is a critical day in a challenging school.' One intra-faith leader, new to headship, described how her compassionate understanding of pupil behavioural problems conflicted with more hard-line views vociferously expressed by a number of staff: 'I had to stand firm on the principles of my faith: my belief in redemption, renewal and reconciliation. I had to bare my soul about this, which was a frightening thing to do, but I gained respect by so doing.' Although the memory of the situation remained painful, the experience was a 'maturing point': 'I had to grow up quickly as a head, but it was also a turning point for the school,' in showing that 'declared values would actually be delivered in action when the going gets tough.' An extra-faith head teacher echoed this need to stand firm on the non-negotiable foundations of his faith and, having first obtained the support of some key staff, was ultimately able to find the courage to challenge those in opposition to that standpoint: 'Tolerance is what we believe in here, so if you can't go along with these values, should you really be here?'

But there is a cost to such commitment, for courageously standing firm whilst being on the edge can be very emotionally draining for the individual school leader. Nowhere is this seen more strongly than when facing the trauma of pupil death, sometimes sudden, violent or self-inflicted. Then it is necessary for the leader to be calm in the eye of the storm, to offer the school as a community space in which to grieve, whilst standing firm on inner foundations of faith so as to provide compassionate support to those in need. This does not come without personal impact. It is, however, underpinned by a belief that leaders are called to leave themselves vulnerable as fellow human beings, by revealing the same wounds and sufferings as those they seek to serve. By admitting their 'own humanity, vulnerability and lack of answers,' whilst drawing inner strength from 'falling back humbly and questioningly onto the bedrock of faith,' they may, in their own woundedness, become a source of healing for others.[20] Indeed, as one intra-faith school leader who had faced such trauma put it: 'God knows we are not perfect, so it is sinful to pretend otherwise. I am only human,' which provides a refreshing antidote to the Superman approach to school leadership.

Questions for Reflection

- Have you felt *called* to your present role or context? If so, how was that call manifested? How is it presently demonstrated?

- What *connected* networks, professional or otherwise, do you rely on for mutual support? How do you both access—and contribute—to them?

- Can you recall a critical incident or challenging circumstance where you had to remain publicly *committed* to your declared values? What was the *cost* of that commitment for you and how did you meet it?

3

Maintaining Direction

Many school leaders can articulate a strong sense of being called to the role, feel connected in supportive networks when discharging it, and remain committed to a vision of a better future for all those entrusted to their care. In confronting the inevitable pressures of leadership, they may draw on the calm, courageous and compassionate attributes identified in the previous chapter as being particularly necessary in times of crisis. In confronting the challenges of change, they will need wisdom to know when to plant new initiatives and when to uproot those practices which are no longer effective, whilst preserving dignity and respect for those bruised by the process, so that the community can continue to live well together and maintain its collective hope.

This chapter seeks to provide a theological scaffolding around these professional attributes. It utilizes the concepts of *logos*, *ethos* and *kairos* as key constituents in maintaining the direction of travel towards *telos*, the looked-for goal. It will show how this model can accommodate the four basic elements of wisdom, hope, community and dignity identified in the *Church of England Vision for Education*, to achieve the ultimate goal of 'life in all its fullness,' not only for students but for school leaders themselves.

Logos

Logos is the Greek term for word, reason or plan. In Christian theology however, the *logos* is the word of God. It reveals the divine reason and plan for our world, it orders it and gives it form and meaning. It is the wisdom that Old Testament prophets and psalmists spoke of as the divine agent which draws human beings into a closer relationship with God, embodied and revealed in the person and example of Jesus Christ: 'the Word made flesh' (John 1.14).

In times of change, the wisdom to be found in the *logos* can provide the right reason for leadership actions, clarity and consistency in the application of values, and succour in times of need. It underpins a sense of calling, reinforces a sense of purpose and provides security amidst the storm. It offers a coherent narrative story which makes the abstract accessible. It provides a yardstick against which to judge the introduction of new initiatives and the discarding of others, assessing what to sow or what to reap. It permits a standard of comparison against the Christian commandment to 'love God and love your neighbour as yourself' (Matt 22.37–39).

For Christians, Jesus Christ is the living *logos*: his life, teaching and example the source of wisdom. However, in an off-piste extension of the concept of *logos*, Sullivan noted that for a commercial company, a logo provides an easily recognized visual image which acts as a 'compressed meaning bearer' to symbolize the essentials of the organization and its products.[21] So school leaders are called to be living logos, providing an embodied form of communication of what their school really stands for and the significance of its work. As living logos they are committed to transmit meaning and values even in the most apparently mundane of activities; they 'live and breathe the second commandment'; they follow the advice of St Francis to 'preach the gospel and if necessary, use words'; or, in modern management parlance, they 'walk the walk, as well as talk the talk.'[22]

Ethos

If *logos* is the seedbed of wisdom from which new initiatives can germinate, then *ethos* is the climate of community which allows them to flourish and grow. Although the term originally comes from the Greek word for custom, it is now used to describe: 'the specific culture of unconsciously learned dispositions, assumptions, values, skills and ways of acting…that have been acquired through the activities and experiences of everyday life.'[23] In other words, it is the lived experience of the totality of daily life in a school or, put more succinctly, simply 'the way we do things round here.'

Ethos is the climate of community which allows new initiatives to flourish and grow

The development and maintenance of *ethos* thus requires both leadership and collectively secured engagement. Leadership is not merely the exercising of authority: it should also be a process of influence in ensuring that the school's declared mission and vision are translated into reality through consistent practice and caring compassionate relationships. This leadership by influence is enhanced by development of strong, connected interpersonal relationships. These are particularly needed when facing challenging circumstances, 'when all seems to be in constant crisis and when strategic direction seems to be swamped by short-term emergencies, for it is then that leaders need to focus on core values and moral purpose.' Utilizing the power of many to build sustainable collective leadership ensures doing the right thing, in the right way rather than just doing the thing right.[24]

Such meaningful, collective engagement can only be secured when a community of people subscribe to agreed common values and to a shared vision, one to which they feel they have contributed and can continue so to do. A primary head teacher sums this up well:

…it's about the whole interaction, the whole level of engagement at all levels…the whole culture and ethos and values of the school are lived, not just taught and planned on a piece of paper…it's fair and accessible to everyone, nobody's disregarded, nobody's isolated, everyone is involved.[25]

Kairos

'For everything there is a season' (Eccl 3.1). Recognition of this is particularly important in the management of change, of deciding when is the critical or opportune moment to sow new initiatives or to cut back on those which have outlived their usefulness. *Kairos* is the Greek word for opportunity, the right time for action. For the Christian, the capacity to read the signs of the times and discern the appropriate moment, the acceptable time, is the generous gift of God's grace (2 Cor 6.1–2).

For many, there is often a recognition of being called to be 'in the right place at the right time' and being 'given the grace to respond appropriately by doing the right thing.' One school leader, facing the trauma of a pupil's sudden death, felt that, 'The community looked to me…we had to gather, we couldn't not gather. I had to invite them in (the parents at the gate), for I was meant to be here for this situation.' In these and more prosaic situations, school leaders of faith have drawn sustenance from an inner self-belief that what they were doing was right, and so felt able 'to put your feet in the right place at the right time and have the courage to stand firm.'

But it is not just in moments of crisis management that such grace is required. It is not simply a question of doing the right thing at the right time, but of also doing it in the right way. Diversity of opinion commands an audience; sincerity of viewpoint demands respect. The timing of change needs to take compassionate account of the impact of that change on those affected by it. Some will mourn the passing of long-held ways of doing things, others will dance at the prospect of new opportunities being offered (Eccl 3.4). For leaders, there will be a time to act and a time to hold back; a time to speak out and a time to remain silent; a time to stand firm and a time to move on.

Telos

If *logos* is the articulation of 'the tale of the loving purposes of God' and its manifestation in the person of Jesus Christ, then *telos* (from the Greek 'complete') is the fulfilment of that purpose.[26] Leaders are called to aspire, plan and act with that 'loving purpose, that ultimate goal, always in sight. This requires them to be endgame driven, weighing the moral worth of proposed actions in the present against their contribution to the achievement of that future goal. It demands a moral compass to maintain the appropriate direction of travel, moral confidence to articulate it, and professional courage to sustain it in ways that remain ethically consistent with that long-term purpose. Above all, as one church-school head teacher succinctly observed, it requires leaders 'to set the problems of school in the perspective of eternity.'

The wisdom to be found in the *logos*, nurtured in a community living well together in an *ethos* of dignity and respect for one another, and implemented at the appropriate time (*kairos*), will reinforce 'our certain hope in God's future for the world, in God's ongoing love and compassion for all people and the whole of creation, and in God's promise of life in all its fullness.'[27]

'The demands of the future shape the present.'[28] For school leaders of whatever faith, planning and action, whilst focused on the present, must therefore constantly have in mind managing the direction of travel towards the ultimate goal (*telos*) of opening up that life in all its fullness for all those entrusted to their care.

Questions for Reflection

- Does Sullivan's concept of 'living logos' resonate for you? If so, what examples of it can you cite from your own leadership practice?

- 'Ethos cannot easily be measured but it can be felt.' What would a visitor to your school feel was its ethos?

- Initiatives need to be introduced at the right time (*kairos*) if their success is to be maximized. Was there a situation for you where it was clearly the wrong time? How did you recover from it?

4 Examining Ethos

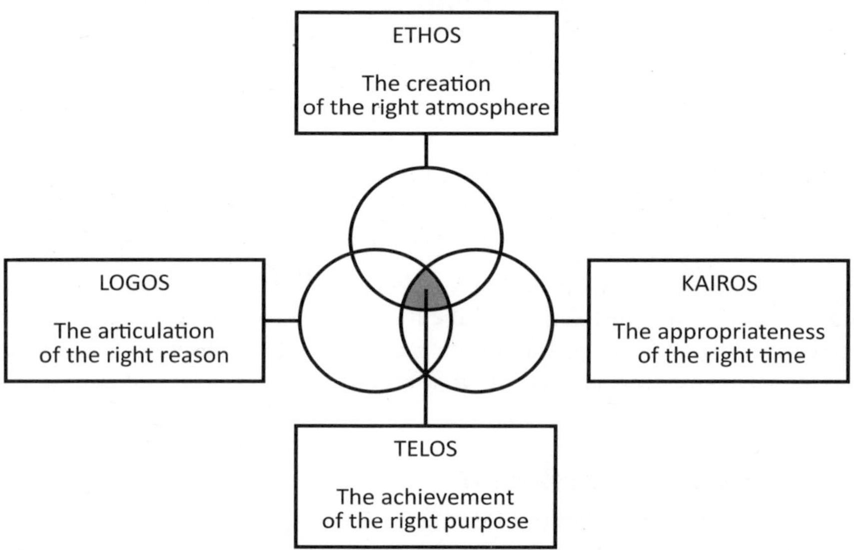

Of the three factors that drive a school forward to achieving its ultimate purpose—*logos, ethos* and *kairos*—ethos is arguably the most important yet the most elusive to define. It has been said that 'Ethos is the ghost in the machine in education. Everyone recognizes it when they see it, parents want it; politicians are in awe of it…'[30] Indeed David Blunkett, when Secretary of State for Education, famously told a conference of Anglican Diocesan Directors of Education in 1998 that church schools had an ethos he wished could be 'bottled' in order to be released into other schools.[31] However, given the multi-faceted nature of ethos, precise delineation of the different compositions of its bottled vintages remains somewhat problematic. Notwithstanding the fact that a visitor entering a school will often fairly quickly make a judgment about the general feel of the place, definition of its actual ethos often remains somewhat nebulous.

Ethos is broader than simply organizational culture; it has been described as 'a pervasive mood which…derives from a shared history of social interactions.'[32] That mood arises out of a shared set of values, agreed by sponsors, governors and senior leaders. It is articulated and promulgated by them, but constrained or amplified by the way staff and students engage with and implement those values on a day-to-day basis. Ethos must be collectively owned and acknowledged as the heart and soul of the school community, but crucially must also be seen to be delivered in action in 'the way we do things around here.'

Establishing the Ethos

Ethos, and engagement with it, was examined by drawing on interviews and fieldwork observations from a small sample of seven Church of England secondary academies linked to a single academy chain, and supplemented by additional later work with three other secondary academies, resulting in a total sample of ten.[33] Although these were all schools of a similar religious character, and the headteachers interviewed were all school leaders of faith, their personal practice spanned a range of faith perspectives: Anglican (4), Roman Catholic (4), United Reformed Church (1), Humanist (1). The schools all served areas of significant social challenge and many were young foundations, replacing earlier institutions deemed to be failing. In this specific context, these particular head teachers had been appointed to turn round and transform the situation by establishing an appropriate ethos and securing engagement with it from the whole school community. Interviews thus sought to gain an understanding of each school's distinctive ethos, where it came from, and what drove and delivered it in practice.

All the schools in the sample fulfilled the requirement to be 'distinctively and recognisably Christian institutions,'[34] with distinctiveness demonstrated in a commitment to put spiritual development at the heart of the curriculum, and a recognisably Christian ethos through the application of clearly ascribed Christian values.[35] All could point to explicit vision statements or ethos statements, which were prominently displayed. In a majority of these, the phrase 'for all faiths and none' was an incessantly recurring mantra. This was sometimes amplified as: 'We are a Christian school but not necessarily just for Christian people,' or underpinned by explicitly Christian references: 'seeing the face of Christ in every child as unique and loved by God,' or by implicit allusion to Christian values focusing on 'redemption not retribution,' with 'freedom to make mistakes and be forgiven.'

Although the schools studied were all Church of England academies, their ethos statements spanned a wide spectrum. One school with a head teacher from a humanist perspective clearly stated that 'inclusivity and high expectations are integral to the school's ethos and mission to promote British values relating to democracy, the rule of law, tolerance and individual liberty,' but did not root these values in explicit Christian antecedents.[36] However, another school, whose Roman Catholic head teacher 'defiantly rejected' the 'here for all faiths and none creed,' made the Christian ethos far more explicit in its prospectus: 'We see education as an integral part of the mission of the church to proclaim all that is good in human living. For students of the Christian faith the Academy aims to provide an environment in which that faith may grow,' whilst recognizing a wider responsibility: 'For students who choose not to follow the Christian faith, the school aims to provide a positive experience of Christianity so that the faith of Christianity might be respected and understood.'

Embedding the Ethos

The sustaining example of the head teacher's own faith demonstrated in practice was significant, not only in establishing ethos but also in embedding it in practice. The *Dearing Report* stressed the need for leaders not just to articulate but also to live out the values they were trying to embed.[37] One head teacher admitted that 'a lot of the ethos came through me and my faith,' with a member of his staff spontaneously praising him as being 'effusively charismatic, leading by example to cascade, embed and eternalize [sic] those values throughout the school.' Another head teacher felt ethos was best maintained 'not in formalized structures but in my management by walking about' and 'through the myriad of daily leadership decisions which, filtered through my faith, connect the fine words on a laminated ethos statement with the gritty realities of school life.' However, embedding ethos is not something solely for the leader. A member of support staff told of 'a lonely and distressed child on transition day being comforted within twenty seconds by an older pupil before I could even get there,' thus demonstrating how students have embraced the school's caring ethos.

Just as important, therefore, as actually establishing the ethos was ensuring that it was embedded across the school in its day-to-day practices. In one school, a member of support staff felt that development of its ethos—and particularly the raising of aspirations and the promotion of equality of opportunity—was 'down to the head…the school wouldn't be the same without him.' However, a community governor in the same school appreciated that the ethos was so embedded that 'if the orchestra conductor were to walk from the stage, the music would carry on, at least for a while.'

This collaborative imperative can be illustrated using an image from Clive James, who in his book *The Fire of Joy* explains that its title comes from the French term, *feu de joie*.[38] This is a military celebration where all a regiment's riflemen each fire a single shot, one after another in quick succession, so that the sound is continuous, like a drum roll. James suggests that symbolically, the 'fire of joy' is a reminder that an organization's collective power relies on the individual and *vice versa*. Each action, however small in itself, is necessary for the final success of the whole. So, although the ethos of a school may be established and choreographed by its leadership, it is sustained by the actions of individuals. As one school leader has observed, 'The ethos may be set by the head teacher but it needs to be "owned" by all the staff if it is to have an impact on the school's distinctiveness.'[39]

The ethos of a school is sustained by the actions of individuals

Engaging with the Ethos

The personal faith commitment of senior leaders informs how they interact: with each other, with fellow members of staff, with students and with the wider community. But it is imperative to secure 'buy in' to the ethos and its underpinning values, to ensure that all staff are willing to operate fully within its parameters. This is sometimes problematic when the faith composition of staff is not uniform. In one school, the staff were a mixture of a minority of active Christians and a minority of non-believers, together with a majority of cultural Christians. Nevertheless, they were all able to articulate—and exemplify in their professional practice—the core Christian values of the school, demonstrating a strong sense of shared fellowship in applying them. There was a ready acceptance that Christian values underpinned the work of the school; however, it was appreciated that these were 'not in your face' but present in 'an ethos of acceptance,' revealed in an open-mindedness 'which respects all faiths and none' and allowed all to operate and flourish within it.[40]

However, it is not simply the staff of a school who need to own the ethos but students, parents and the wider community too. Potential leadership mechanisms for enhancing the strength of such engagement have been identified and developed using a dynamic networking approach, as detailed in the Church of England Foundation for Educational Leadership publication, *Ethos Enhancing Outcomes*.[41] Increased student engagement with an improved ethos has been shown to generate small but significant quantitative improvement in both levels of overall attendance and GCSE academic outcomes.[42]

But as important, if not more so, was the effect on life-enhancing pastoral outcomes. One parent of a student with special educational needs valued the inclusive and individualized child-centred focus embedded in the ethos, and the recognition that 'all are not judged here simply on a Richter scale of brilliance.' Some students in schools serving areas of particularly high social deprivation, where there was perceived to be 'little parental moral steerage,' valued the sense of moral direction the school gave them: 'I was going to do this [risky sexual behaviour] but it made me stop and think. I now know I have a choice, and I'm better prepared to make it,' said one female student, whilst a Year 11 male student searingly asserted: 'I'd be in jail now if it weren't for the academy.'

A former Minister of State for Education once argued, 'Ethos is an incredibly important thing. And the best schools—whether faith schools or not—have understood that and run with it.'[43] Whilst this chapter has focused on research in the secondary church school sector, its findings are surely equally applicable to all schools in all phases. As one primary school head confirmed, 'It is the depth and quality of our ethos that will truly enhance our outcomes today, tomorrow and in the future.'[44]

Questions for Reflection

- How would you describe to a visitor, in no more than a few sentences, the ethos of your school?

- What examples of 'ethos enhancing outcomes' could you advance to demonstrate conversion from 'laminated ethos statement' to application in day-to-day practices? How has your own faith position impacted and sustained you in ensuring this?

- How will you embed your ethos in the 'heart and soul' of new generations of staff and students as they come to join your school?

Securing Change

5

Change is the only constant in life.[45]

Costs of Change

Change may well be regarded as a constant in life, but the fear of change itself, as well as suspicion of its potential costs, is also a constant. That inherent suspicion of change was seen in the responses at some academies studied in the previous chapter, many of whom had emerged from schools deemed to be failing. In one, there was resistance from some students and staff transferred from the predecessor school, who were feeling 'rattled by the change to a more overtly Christian ethos' in an institution lacking resilience and still bruised by fear of failure. This was compounded by a community, traditionally resistant to change, feeling that it had 'Christianity thrust upon it' and who were 'resentful of the shock of the new.' It had required recognition by the head teacher that the school was 'on an incremental journey from turbulence to transformation' and that some of the details of the route would need to be revisited, whilst still maintaining the overall direction of travel. In another academy that was seeking to break a perceived 'cycle of learned helplessness' within the community, there had been belated recognition of the failure by the sponsor at the outset to clarify, demythologize and promulgate the community-focused service mission of the academy to a very disadvantaged area. This had subsequently necessitated a leadership decision to throttle back the overtness of the Christian ethos, so as not to cause unnecessary alarm to parents, community and the majority of staff who were not active Christians.

This tension between a community that placed the provision of a good school as its priority, and a sponsor seeking first the development of a good church school, came at an unsustainable cost for some school leaders. It is significant that in seeking to build a sample of ten academies to be studied, two potential contributor academies had seen their head teachers suspended by the sponsor, whilst two others subsequently suffered the resignation of their head teachers on health grounds. One of the latter, an Anglican, felt 'attacked' by staff and the wider community for her efforts to turn what she felt was 'a church school in name only' into something more worthy of the appellation. Another, a Humanist, felt 'unsupported' by the sponsors when he focused first on securing better academic progress in an area of limited aspiration that had previously lacked such success.

This rate of senior leadership attrition highlights two major messages regarding the management of change. First there is the importance of providing clarity, consistency and constant *reinforcement* of a mutually agreed and collectively owned vision, as well as the intended direction of travel towards it, before embarking on the journey of change itself. Secondly there must be recognition and acceptance that implementation of successful change takes time. Inevitably there will be participants and stakeholders who are bruised by the process of change and who will need *reassurance* and encouragement to embrace it.

Implementation of successful change takes time

Many in teaching may mourn the loss of tried and tested traditional ways of working, or be perturbed by the disturbance to their equilibrium from the shock of the new. Through leadership awareness of possible emotional responses to change, and firm faith in the benefits that will accrue from its implementation, leaders can continue to preserve, for both participants and stakeholders, the key role of hope as a motivational driver towards a better future.

Change of Leaders

Disturbance to equilibrium is often felt within a school community when there is a change in senior leadership. This may be externally imposed or long planned, with existing leaders 'recognizing when it is right to move on.' Colleagues and the wider community will need reassurance: that long-cherished and mutually agreed values and implementation practices will not be arbitrarily overthrown; that any replacement will be an improvement on what has gone on before; and that a direction of travel, long pursued, will not be radically altered without apparent reason. But this is not to argue for stasis. There will also need to be a recognition that a school and its community cannot be set in aspic.

The leader's role will need to change at different stages of the school's development, requiring different emphases on different professional strengths at different times.[46] 'Heroic' leaders appointed to a school to rescue it from persistent underachievement will need to morph into consolidator leaders, who provide the steady hand on the tiller to see the changes through and secure them in day-to-day operational practice. Equally, 'pruner' leaders, who cut away some previous developments which have outlived their usefulness in order to make room for growth of new initiatives, may need also to become 'nurturer' leaders who rebuild fractured relationships and bruised professional morale as a consequence of such change. Throughout it all, there must be leaders with a consistency of vision, who have the faith to be able to see the wood for the trees in terms of the school's potential for long-term development, accompanied by an extended change plan for fulfilling it.

Even if there is no actual change in leadership personnel, there may thus need to be *readjustment* of leadership style to respond to changes in circumstance. Leaders may need to draw on the wisdom of one secondary head teacher who had been in post in the same school for over twenty years: 'One of the secrets of leadership longevity is a seemingly limitless capacity to reinvent oneself as the school has developed.'

Leaders of Change

The key role of the leader in driving change forward must be the sustaining of hope. The leader must acknowledge the emotional journey that colleagues are experiencing, encourage them to take the leap of faith into new territory, and reinforce in word and deed throughout the process that the envisaged change remains true to fundamental values rooted in the logos and embodied in the ethos of the school. Leaders must recognize when is the right time for a change (*kairos*) and be able to embed it securely within the collective journey towards the hoped-for ultimate end goal (*telos*) of life in all its fullness.

However, if leaders are to effectively drive the process of change, with its incessant demands on time, energy and emotions, they must recognize the need to resource themselves for the journey. They must stand firmly on their own sustaining 'foundations of faith' (whatever they may be) and find ways to replenish their own internal 'reservoir of hope' through reflective, re-energizing and renewing strategies, if they are then to be able to act as the reservoir of hope for others. In essence, 'School leaders are repositories of human hopes and dreams for becoming our better selves, but…if our own reservoirs are empty, there is nothing left for us to give to those we are called to serve.'[47]

'Change is the only constant in life,' but when a leader's capacity to cope with change is tested by challenging circumstances, conflicting pressures and a community that might traditionally be resistant to change, they must face the inevitable challenges of change by maintaining a faithful constancy of vision and values, sustained by faith, inspired by hope, and transformed by love. As one primary head teacher summed it up: 'It doesn't matter what government comes in, what education policy or education act comes in, our common mission and values remain…remain steady.'[48]

Questions for Reflection

- Recall a change you were responsible for or heavily involved with. Why was it initiated? How was it implemented? What resistance did you face?

- What emotions did you and those participating in the change go through? How did you deal with them?

- What impacts did the change process have on you as a leader? How did you ensure your inner reservoir of hope was refilled? How did your faith sustain you through the process?

Summing It Up

Leadership should stand firmly on foundations of faith. That faith may be derived from a variety of perspectives and sustained by a multitude of sources. It provides a personal value system, to inspire a vision grounded in faith and to sustain action based upon it. It offers a scaffolding of support and a moral compass to secure direction, particularly in times of challenge and change.

Each of the preceding chapters explored these issues and the findings can be summed up as follows:

- Three leadership characteristics: *called, committed, connected*
- Three leadership descriptors: *calm, courageous, compassionate*
- Three theological imperatives: *logos, ethos, kairos*
- Three facets of ethos: *establishing, embedding, engaging*
- Three conditions for change: *reinforcement, reassurance, readjustment*
- Three essentials for progress: *sustaining faith, inspiring hope, transforming love.*

Notes

1   A J Flintham, *Sustaining Hope in School Leadership* (Grove Education booklet eD22).

2   A J Flintham, *Reservoirs of Hope: Sustaining Spirituality in School Leaders* (Newcastle upon Tyne: Cambridge Scholars Publishing, 2010).

3   Church of England Education Office, *Church of England Vision for Education: Deeply Christian, Serving the Common Good* (London: Church House Publishing, 2016) p 2.

4   *ibid,* p 2.

5   G Davie, *Religion in Britain since 1945: Believing without Belonging* (Oxford: Blackwell, 1994)

6   T Cooling, *Doing God in Education* (London: Theos, 2010) p 15.

7   *ibid,* p 70.

8   G Georgiou, *Religious Literacy in Schools* (Grove Education booklet eD40) p 19, drawing on the Commission on Religious Education, 'Religion and Worldviews: The Way Forward' (2018).

9   A Farnell, *Grow Your Own School Leaders: Learning from Experience in Church Schools* (Grove Education booklet eD35) p 8.

10 A J Flintham, *Reservoirs of Hope, op cit,* p 80. For other taxonomies, see E Spencer and B Lucas, *Christian Leadership in Schools: An initial review of evidence and current practices* (London: Church of England Education Office, Foundation for Educational Leadership, 2019) pp 10–13 and pp 28–37.

11 A J Flintham, *Faith, Hope and Spirituality in School Leaders* (unpublished PhD thesis: University of Liverpool, 2009) p 277, with supplemental interview data 2014–2019.

12 D F Ford and A Wolfe, *Called, Connected, Committed: 24 Leadership Practices for Education Leaders* (London: Church of England Education Office, Foundation for Educational Leadership, 2019).

13 *Church of England Vision for Education, op cit,* p 2.

14 Ford and Wolfe, *Called, Connected, Committed, op cit,* p 2.

15 Archbishops of Canterbury and York, 'Letter to the Nation,' 4 November 2020, https://www.archbishopofcanterbury.org/news/letter-nation-archbishops-canterbury-and-york, accessed 4 November 2020.

16 N Genders, Chief Education Officer's 'Letter to Church of England Schools,' 4 January 2021, https://www.churchofengland.org/news-and-media/news-and-statements/starting-term-amid-covid-19-uncertainty-schools-need, accessed 21 January 2021.

17 Flintham, *Sustaining Hope in School Leadership, op cit,* p 16.

18 S Schumacher, *Reimagining the Spiritual Disciplines for a Digital Age* (Grove Spirituality booklet S153).

19 M de Pree, *Leadership is an Art* (New York: Doubleday, 2004) p 136.

20 H Nouwen, *The Wounded Healer: Ministry in Contemporary Society* (London: Darton, Longman and Todd, 1994) p 82.

21 J Sullivan, 'Living Logos,' in P Boylan (ed), *Networking: Catholic Education Today* 3 (2002) pp 28–31.

22 G James, head teacher, St Mary's Church of England Primary School, Tunstall, Stoke-on-Trent, in 'They dug out the foundations,' Unit 4 of M Buck and G Bradbury (eds), *Leading a Catholic School and Academy* (London: Catholic Education Service, 2014) p 14.

23 A B Morris, 'Some Social Benefits of English Catholic Schools,' *International Studies in Catholic Education* 6:1 (2014) p 87.

24 P Duignan and H Cannon, *The Power of Many: Building Sustainable Collective Leadership in Schools* (Camberwell: Australian Council for Educational Research Press, 2011) p 26.

25 M Yates, head teacher, St Gregory's Catholic Primary School, Longton, Stoke-on-Trent, in Buck and Bradbury (eds), *Leading a Catholic School and Academy, op cit*, p 15.

26 Bidding Prayer, *The Promise of His Glory* (London: Church House Publishing, 1991) p 148.

27 N Genders, *op cit.*

28 L Mlodinow, *Stephen Hawking: A Memoir of Friendship and Physics* (London: Allen Lane, 2020) p 102.

29 H Freiberg, *School Climate: measuring, improving and sustaining healthy learning environments* (London: Falmer, 1999) p 1.

30 M Bunting, 'Faith schools can best generate the common purpose that pupils need,' *The Guardian*, 8 September 2008, https://www.theguardian.com/commentisfree/2008/sep/08/faithschools, accessed 29 December 2020.

31 J Hall, 'We have bottled the Ethos,' *The Church Times*, 7 February 2007, https://www.churchtimes.co.uk/articles/2007/9-february/features/we-have-bottled-the-ethos, accessed 29 December 2020.

32 E Green, *Mapping the Field: a review of the current research evidence on the impact of schools with a Christian ethos* (London: Theos, 2009) p 20.

33 A Flintham, E Green and D Moore, 'A Study of Ethos and Engagement in Seven Church of England Academies,' in A B Morris (ed), *Faith, Hope and Educational Research* (Liverpool: Liverpool Hope University, 2016) pp 107–130.

34 R Dearing, *The Way Ahead: Church of England Schools in the New Millennium* (London: Church House Publishing, 2001) p 2.

35 P Chadwick, *The Church School of the Future Review* (London: Archbishop's Council, Education Division, 2012) p 2.

36 P Draycott, *British Values in Church Schools: Making Them Count* (Grove Education booklet eD29).

37 Dearing, *The Way Ahead, op cit*, p 60.

38 C James, *The Fire of Joy* (London: Picador, 2020) p 1.

39 G Holmes, *To what extent does the head teacher's value system influence the ethos of the Church of England voluntary controlled primary school* (unpublished EdD thesis: Anglia Ruskin University, 2015) p 60.

40 A Flintham, E Green and D Moore, 'A Study of Ethos and Engagement,' in A B Morris (ed), *Faith, Hope and Educational Research, op cit,* p 122.

41 A Wolfe, *Ethos Enhancing Outcomes: Exploring 20 School Leadership Issues* (London: Church of England Education Office, Foundation for Educational Leadership, 2018).

42 R Godfrey and A B Morris, 'The Academic Performance of Church of England Academies,' in A B Morris (ed), *Faith, Hope and Educational Research, op cit,* pp 131–172.

43 J Knight, speech to Catholic Education Service 'Visions for Leadership' Conference, London (31 March 2009), cited in A B Morris, *Catholic Education: Universal Principles, Locally Applied* (Newcastle upon Tyne: Cambridge Scholars Publishing, 2012) p 181.

44 L Dadds, 'Waffles from a Headteacher,' 1 October 2018, https://wafflesofansbl. com/2018/10/01/ethos-enhancing-outcomes/, accessed 5 February 2021.

45 Attributed to Heraclitus, fourth-century BCE Greek philosopher.

46 A J Flintham, 'Post-Modernist Portfolio People: sustainability and succession in school headship,' *Management in Education* 18.3 (2004) pp 16–19, https://journals.sagepub.com/doi/abs/10.1177/0892020604018003047journalCode=miea

47 P Kidson, 'Connect, disconnect, and reconnect: imperatives for reflective school leaders,' 22 September 2017, https://www.linkedin.com/pulse/connect-disconnect-reconnect-imperatives-reflective-school-kidson, accessed 7 February 2021.

48 M Yates in Buck and Bradbury, *Leading a Catholic School and Academy, op cit,* p 19.